99 HISTORIES

BY JULIA CHO

★

★

DRAMATISTS
PLAY SERVICE
INC.

NOTE ON BILLING

Anyone receiving permission to produce 99 HISTORIES is required to give credit to the Author as sole and exclusive Author of the Play on the title page of all programs distributed in connection with performances of the Play and in all instances in which the title of the Play appears, including printed or digital materials for advertising, publicizing or otherwise exploiting the Play and/or a production thereof. The name of the Author must appear on a separate line, in which no other name appears, immediately beneath the title and in size of type equal to 50% of the size of the largest, most prominent letter used for the title of the Play. No person, firm or entity may receive credit larger or more prominent than that accorded the Author. The following acknowledgments must appear on the title page of all programs distributed in connection with performances of the Play:

Originally developed by Cherry Lane Theatre, Mentor Project 2002,
Angelina Fiordellisi, Artistic Director.
Subsequently produced at Theatre Mu in Minneapolis, MN.

Developed with the assistance of the
Sundance Institute Theatre Laboratory
and workshopped at South Coast Repertory
and the Mark Taper Forum's Asian Theatre Workshop.

SPECIAL NOTE ON SONGS/RECORDINGS

Dramatists Play Service neither holds the rights to nor grants permission to use any songs or recordings mentioned in the Play. Permission for performances of copyrighted songs, arrangements or recordings mentioned in this Play is not included in our license agreement. The permission of the copyright owner(s) must be obtained for any such use. For any songs and/or recordings mentioned in the Play, other songs, arrangements, or recordings may be substituted provided permission from the copyright owner(s) of such songs, arrangements or recordings is obtained; or songs, arrangements or recordings in the public domain may be substituted.

For my parents, James Cho and Sun Hui Cho

Heartfelt thanks to John Buzzetti, Michael Greif,
Jessica Kubzansky, Leigh Silverman and Chay Yew

99 HISTORIES was originally produced by the Cherry Lane Theatre (Angelina Fiordellisi, Founding Artistic Director) in New York City, opening on April 23, 2002. It was directed by Maria Mileaf; the set design was by Nathan Heverin; the costume design was by Soonwha Choi; the lighting design was by Nicole Pearce; the sound design was by Matthew T. Lebe; the prop design was by Faye Armon; the production stage manager was J.J. Lee; the assistant stage manager was Kate Greenberg; the associate producer was Tracy S. Johnson; and the production manager was Chime Serra. The cast was as follows:

EUNICE .... Elaina Erika Davis
SAH-JIN .... Mia Katigbak
GIRL .... Ann Hu
DANIEL MERRITT/JOE .... Daniel Pettie
YOUNG WOMAN .... Mia Tagano
PAUL .... Joel de la Fuente

99 HISTORIES was subsequently produced by Intermedia Arts (David Gumnit, Executive Director) and Theatre Mu (Rick Shiomi, Artistic Director) in Minneapolis, Minnesota, opening on April 9, 2004. It was directed by Cecilie D. Keenan; the assistant director was Mary Beidler Gearen; the set design was by Rick Paul; the costume design was by Malia Burkhart; the lighting design was by Mike Grogan; the sound design was by Dixie Treichel; the prop design was by Roxanne Skarphol; and the stage manager was Melanie Salmon-Peterson. The cast was as follows:

EUNICE .... Jeany Park
SAH-JIN .... Maria Cheng
GIRL/YOUNG SAH-JIN .... Cindy Koy
DANIEL MERRITT/JOE .... Sean Logan
YOUNG WOMAN .... Sara Ochs
PAUL .... Tae-Jung Kwan

99 HISTORIES was developed with the assistance of the Sundance Institute Theatre Laboratory, South Coast Repertory, New York Theater Workshop, the Mark Taper Forum's Asian Theatre Workshop and the Cherry Lane Alternative.

CHARACTERS

EUNICE: Female, Korean-American, late twenties.

SAH-JIN: Female, American-Korean, Eunice's mother, fifties.

GIRL / YOUNG SAH-JIN: Female, Korean-American.

DANIEL MERRITT: Male, white American, twenties.

YOUNG WOMAN: Female, Korean, twenty.

JOE: Male, white American. Played by the actor who plays Daniel.

PAUL: Male, Korean-American, early thirties.

SETTING

A suburb of Los Angeles.

NOTE

The scenes are fluid and run into each other, with only occasional brief beats. Keep in mind that scenes have different textures: some are memories, some are dreams, some are everyday realities. The shifts in texture should be reflected somehow, whether it's through a change in lighting, pacing or tone.

99 HISTORIES

PROLOGUE

The sound of a cello. A young girl plays like a master. Sah-Jin sits with her eyes closed, listening. The girl stops and looks at her hands.

SAH-JIN. What is it?
GIRL. *(Touching her fingertips.)* Hurts.
SAH-JIN. Keep playing. It will go away.
GIRL. I sound awful.
SAH-JIN. No. Beautiful.
GIRL. Bach would turn over in his grave.
SAH-JIN. Someday you can be better than Bach.
GIRL. Don't be ridiculous.
SAH-JIN. Better than Casals. Better than Yo-Yo Ma.
GIRL. *(Thinks about it.)* Maybe.
SAH-JIN. I tell you, you can be anything you want. If you don't get what you want …
SAH-JIN and GIRL. … it just means you didn't want it bad enough.
SAH-JIN. Words become reality.
GIRL. I know.
SAH-JIN. Then again. *(The girl plays. The lights dim.)*

ACT ONE

Scene 1

Eunice's bedroom. Eunice stands still in the middle of the room. Sah-Jin moves quickly around her. Sah-Jin's hair is swept back in a tight bun. She turns down the bed.

EUNICE. I told you I can sleep on the sofa bed, I don't mind.
SAH-JIN. It's *your* room.
EUNICE. I don't want to be a bother.
SAH-JIN. What bother? *(Sah-Jin opens the closet. She takes out a pillow and a shoebox. She throws the pillow on the bed and hands Eunice the box.)* Here.
EUNICE. What's this?
SAH-JIN. I just saw and thought you would like. *(Eunice opens the box and holds up a very fancy, black high-heeled shoe.)* That's a good brand, very comfortable.
EUNICE. Yeah, they'll go really well with my sleek maternity fashion.
SAH-JIN. Why are you like this?
EUNICE. Like what?
SAH-JIN. Bitter. Just put it on.
EUNICE. *(Putting on a shoe.)* I am *not* bitter. I am *sarcastic*. There's a difference.
SAH-JIN. *(Admiring the shoe.)* I knew they'd fit.
EUNICE. They're too nice for me.
SAH-JIN. How can you say that? Anyway, I got them on sale.
EUNICE. Where are you going?
SAH-JIN. Service.
EUNICE. Now?
SAH-JIN. Saturday evening service. I play the piano and I'm the alto.
EUNICE. *The* alto?
SAH-JIN. Unless you want to join —
EUNICE. Forget it, I'm not going.
SAH-JIN. Okay.

EUNICE. That's it? No fighting? No pleading?
SAH-JIN. You're a grown woman. If you don't want to go, don't go. Anyway, the people at church don't know you're here. It would just be awkward.
EUNICE. Oh, I'd embarrass you.
SAH-JIN. That is *not* what I said —
EUNICE. Just what do you tell your friends about me?
SAH-JIN. The truth. That you travel a lot. For your. Work.
EUNICE. Good one! They probably think I'm a flight attendant.
SAH-JIN. What I don't understand is, if you like travel so much, why *not* just work for an airline and be something, anything, not just a, a —
EUNICE. Bum?
SAH-JIN. Yes, *bum*. I'm just saying, I didn't even know you were in New York. I thought you were still in Boston. How terrible, own mother not knowing where you are.
EUNICE. I got tired of Boston.
SAH-JIN. Your postcard said you liked it.
EUNICE. Of course it did, it was a *postcard*.
SAH-JIN. I hate those.
EUNICE. Would you rather I didn't write at all?
SAH-JIN. You could call.
EUNICE. I meant to.
SAH-JIN. Meant to is one thing, Eunice. Done is another. I am not embarrassed about you but you — you tell me nothing, about where you are, where you been. I just get a phone call, out of the blue, suddenly I have a daughter again. And you know what she's saying? Not, "Hello, I miss you," not, "How are you." She's saying, "Hi, Ma, it's me, I don't have AIDS."
EUNICE. You were the one who told me when I left home, "Don't get AIDS and don't get pregnant." I was just trying to ease you into the news.
SAH-JIN. Oh, Eunice.
EUNICE. I'm sorry, okay? I didn't know what to say, I didn't know *how* to say.
SAH-JIN. I am not ashamed of you, but there are some things that are private and some things that are public. *This* is private.
EUNICE. And what is private, you hide, right?
SAH-JIN. You're the one come home to hide. I'm not a foolish old woman, Eunice-yah. I know you haven't come home for me. *(Pause.)*

EUNICE. So were you surprised to hear from me?
SAH-JIN. Not surprised. Shocked. But then I see this nature show, on the satellite TV, about salmon and then I think I understand better.
EUNICE. You bought a satellite dish? We never even had cable.
SAH-JIN. I can watch shows from Korea now, but that is not the point. Point is, salmon are born in one pool and then live their whole life somewhere else. But then they come back. They swim against the water, upstream, you know how hard that is? Just so they can come back to where they were born. Like you.
EUNICE. Yeah, and then they die.
SAH-JIN. I'm just saying, you may not know why you're home, but you're like those fish. Something happens, you feel the tug and you come home. No choice. You come home — there's rice in the kitchen, don't forget to eat.
EUNICE. I won't.
SAH-JIN. And if you want to help you can finish cleaning up the room. I'll do the laundry when I get home. Or you can do it. Do some work at home for a change. *(Sah-Jin leaves. The lights shift. Joe appears. He doesn't have a shirt on. He is holding an iron.)*
JOE. Eunice. Hey.
EUNICE. Is this a bad time? If it's a bad time, I can —
JOE. It's fine. Just talk to me while I get ready. *(They are in his apartment. He starts ironing his shirt.)*
EUNICE. How've you been?
JOE. Good, good. Things are good. You?
EUNICE. Good.
JOE. Well that's ... good. Guess who I ran into? At the post office? Janet.
EUNICE. Which one's Janet?
JOE. I told you about her. She was before. You never met her. Anyway, turns out she's moved to a place on Seventh. So we're going to hang out.
EUNICE. Is it a date? You don't have to answer that.
JOE. We're just friends. She's got a boyfriend, a serious one.
EUNICE. How do you do that?
JOE. Do what?
EUNICE. Stay friends with all of your exes.
JOE. I don't know. Breaking up doesn't change who you are. You still like who that person is, right? And Janet's great. I mean, when

you think about it, it hasn't even been that long since she and I broke up. Year and a half. That's not long at all.
EUNICE. For some people it isn't. *(Joe finishes ironing. He shakes the shirt and then puts it on.)*
JOE. I read somewhere that it takes a year to shed one entire layer of skin. So when you think about it that way, it's a whole year before you lose the layer of skin that holds the memory of someone, the touch of someone. *(He leaves the room.)*
EUNICE. *(Softly.)* Where does your skin hold the memory of me? *(Joe reenters holding a tie in each hand.)*
JOE. A or B? A … B. Neither. You hate them both.
EUNICE. No.
JOE. Then why the face?
EUNICE. Look, I had to run some errands in the neighborhood and just thought I'd stop by and return these. Keys. I thought maybe you'd want them back. *(She digs into her pocket and hands him a ring of keys.)*
JOE. I thought you lost these.
EUNICE. Yeah, but I was cleaning and I guess they'd fallen back behind —
JOE. What do you mean you were "cleaning"?
EUNICE. I was putting things away…? Dusting?
JOE. You hate cleaning. I've seen you. You get nervous when things get too organized.
EUNICE. Yeah, well, I was packing some stuff up and I —
JOE. Packing? You're moving.
EUNICE. No. Kind of. Just subletting. I'll only be gone a little bit.
JOE. Where?
EUNICE. L.A.
JOE. What? Why?
EUNICE. You sound like a newspaper article, where, what, when …
JOE. Eunice.
EUNICE. It's just for a little while, just to see my mother.
JOE. Your mother. You told me your parents were dead.
EUNICE. I told you my *father* was dead. My mother, she's. She's in L.A.
JOE. Did something happen? Is she sick?
EUNICE. No, nothing like that.
JOE. Then what?
EUNICE. I don't know. You always got a reason for what you do?
JOE. Yes.

EUNICE. I don't always know if I do.
JOE. Well, let's start small. Why are you here? *(Eunice doesn't say anything.)* All right. I'm out. You know what your problem is? You're like Russia.
EUNICE. What's that supposed to mean?
JOE. It's like when Napoleon went to war with Russia. He amasses this huge army and drives into Russian territory, hungry to fight. He can't wait. So he gets his men ready and then the next morning, he goes out to the battlefield and charges the enemy. Except the field is totally empty. There isn't a Russian to be seen. He keeps chasing them farther and farther into the interior, and they just keep withdrawing until finally Napoleon and his men are starving and exhausted and defeated.
EUNICE. So I'm a big land mass?
JOE. Exactly.
EUNICE. Well, why didn't you tell me we were at war.
JOE. I am not your enemy.
EUNICE. You were the one who called me Russia!
JOE. I'm just saying that you have a habit of doing that. Withdrawing. You know I tried. Even when we were together, I always felt alone. And I'd only brought so many supplies with me and they only lasted so long.
EUNICE. I know. You don't have to say. *(A small silence.)* Listen. You want to hear a story?
JOE. Is it scary? It looks scary.
EUNICE. No, funny. I went to the doctor the other day and you know how they make you pee in those little cups? I'm in the bathroom and you know usually you never see any graffiti in those bathrooms, they're always squeaky clean, right? But there I am, on the toilet, staring at the door and there's something written on it. Someone had scratched the words right into the metal, like with a key. And it said:

Hit me
hurt me
call me Eileen.

Except there wasn't any punctuation. I couldn't figure out if it was a directive *to* an Eileen: "Hit me, hurt me, call me, *(Brief pause.)* Eileen," or a directive in general: "Hit me, hurt me, call me Eileen." It's been driving me crazy. I can't do anything but meditate on the various states of Eileen.

JOE. That's funny.
EUNICE. Uh huh.
JOE. So why were you at the doctor's?
EUNICE. It reminds me of a joke, you know, one of those name jokes? What do you call a girl with one leg?
JOE. Eunice, why were you at —
EUNICE. No, not Eunice. Another name. Come on. Answer. Guess.
JOE. I don't know.
EUNICE. Eileen. You call her Eileen. Get it? *(She looks at him. He's not laughing.)*
JOE. Why — were — you —
EUNICE. Well, hit me, hurt me, call me Eileen, I'm pregnant, Joe. *(A long, awful pause.)*
JOE. I thought we were — ?
EUNICE. We were.
JOE. Then how?
EUNICE. I don't know.
JOE. How long?
EUNICE. Four weeks.
JOE. That's not a very long time.
EUNICE. For some people it isn't. *(Pause.)*
JOE. Have you thought about — ? I mean, are you going to — ?
EUNICE. Adoption. I decided on adoption.
JOE. You're sure that's what you want?
EUNICE. Well, I can't … so is there any other option? *(Pause.)* Didn't think so.
JOE. Eunice, you can't just spring this on me and then disappear to California. What am I supposed to do with that?
EUNICE. I have no choice. Don't you understand?
JOE. Do you need money, is that it? How much?
EUNICE. No, no. I don't want anything from you.
JOE. But I want to —
EUNICE. No. The agency will pay for the — it's all worked out, you don't have to. That's why I'm going home, just until … It's fine. It's like the prodigal son always said, right? There's no place like home.
JOE. That was Dorothy.
EUNICE. Whatever. The thing about home is it always takes you back — rent-free.
JOE. Stop making jokes.
EUNICE. *(Defensively.)* What. I'm sorry. I'm just so bad at this.

JOE. Adoption.
EUNICE. Yeah. It really is for the best. I have thought about it. A lot.
JOE. I just. Need some time to think, okay? Will you call me? From L.A.?
EUNICE. Sure. *(They both know she won't.)*
JOE. You call me if you need anything.
EUNICE. Okay, Napoleon.
JOE. What's your number there?
EUNICE. When I call I'll give it to you. *(Pause.)* I should get going.
JOE. I'll walk you out.
EUNICE. No, it's okay. You go wherever you need, take your time.
JOE. I'm glad you told me.
EUNICE. Well, that was always the thing, right? I could always tell you anything.
JOE. You could. But you hardly ever did. *(Joe is gone.)*

Scene 2

Eunice sits, writing. It's very late.

EUNICE. Dear … whatsyourname.
To Whom It May Concern, I was your mother, no.
To … you.
To you.
I know you're hoping for some kind of epiphany or revelation. Well, I have nothing like that for you. The simple fact is, I was not made for you. That mother smell, that softness. I wasn't made for that. I was just a temp on Wall Street, a sad-faced, pale little office worker like Bartleby the scrivener, looking out a window that faced only a wall. Speaking of which, optional reading list, books I like: "Bartleby, the Scrivener," Melville.
As for where you come from … well, there isn't much to tell. I come from a family that doesn't really talk about the past. For instance, my mother has a scar on her throat but I still don't know exactly how she got it. When I was a kid, I thought she said it was

a "star," and so for most of my growing up, I thought she had some magic in her, right there, shaped like a mini-explosion.

I remember once, when I was in eighth grade, I had to make a family tree as a class project. *(Visual of a diagram with very few boxes and a lot of white space.)* Me. Only child. My father with two half-brothers I've never met. My mother: one sister who died when she was just a child. My father's parents, my mother's parents — grandfathers dead on both sides before I was even born. And that's it. Ta-Dah.

I took this chart to school, very proud of what I had done. And who was up first, but my best friend, Liz Grady. *(Visual of a diagram with boxes and lines branching out in wild proliferation.)* Her family tree was the size of a Volvo. She had people like Anne Boleyn, George Washington. Liz Grady oozed history. She once showed me the contents of her hope chest: linens from her grandmother, silver from her great-aunt, stuff that had been passed down for generations. I looked at it and thought to myself: I have no hope chest. I have no hope.

I'm just saying, so what if you grew up not knowing where you were from? Maybe more than hair color or eye shape, it's that feeling that proves you are mine.

Scene 3

Late afternoon the next day. Sah-Jin and Paul are sitting at the dining table. Above the table is a faded photo of Eunice's father when he was impossibly young and good-looking. Eunice enters. She is still in her pajamas.

SAH-JIN. Eunice-ya! There you are. You've been hiding in your room all day. Dinner's ready. And look who's here. *(Paul stands up and offers his hand. Eunice is dumbfounded.)*
PAUL. Hey, I'm Paul. Your mom's told me a lot about you.
EUNICE. That's. Great. Mom.
SAH-JIN. I've been meaning to invite Paul and his sister over to dinner, but the one night we all get around to it, she has to work! But at least Paul could make it.

PAUL. I don't get home cooking like this very often.
EUNICE. She didn't make any of it. It comes in containers from the Korean supermarket.
SAH-JIN. Eunice.
PAUL. Well, it's still delicious.
SAH-JIN. *(To Eunice.)* Sit. *(To Paul.)* You'll have to excuse how she's dressed. She hasn't been feeling well lately.
PAUL. Sorry to hear it. How're you feeling now?
EUNICE. Nauseous, thanks for asking.
SAH-JIN. She's really not usually like this.
EUNICE. It's just the pregnancy —
SAH-JIN. Eunice!
EUNICE. — morning sickness and all.
PAUL. Maybe I can help.
SAH-JIN. Paul's a doctor.
EUNICE. Well of course he is!
SAH-JIN. That's enough. Was that the phone?
EUNICE. I didn't hear —
SAH-JIN. I'll get it! You two talk, get to know each other. *(Sah-Jin leaves. Paul and Eunice sit in awkward silence. Finally, Paul picks up his chopsticks and begins to eat. Eunice watches Paul eat. She can't take it anymore; she picks up her chopsticks and starts eating too. She realizes she's ravenous.)*
PAUL. Good, huh? *(Eunice nods.)*
EUNICE. Can you hand me that stuff?
PAUL. The kong-na-mul? *(She nods. He hands a dish to her.)*
EUNICE. Thanks. So how'd my mom rope you into dinner?
PAUL. She didn't. I like her. She's so funny.
EUNICE. Funny?
PAUL. She's always giving me food in Tupperware, like she thinks I'm starving. It's like, "Eat! How are you? Eat!" My mom passed away about ten years ago. When I started coming to your mom's church, she kind of adopted me. She's really sweet.
EUNICE. Are we talking about the same person?
PAUL. Don't be so hard on her.
EUNICE. Am I? Hard on her?
PAUL. Kind of.
EUNICE. She never mentioned you.
PAUL. Well, from what I gather, you two don't talk very often. She says you're off traveling a lot.

EUNICE. Yeah.
PAUL. You don't remember me at all, do you?
EUNICE. What?
PAUL. We went to the same church, back in junior high.
EUNICE. I don't think so.
PAUL. No, I'm pretty sure.
EUNICE. Really?
PAUL. Yeah, we all knew who you were. All the kids. We'd talk about you and be like, "That damn Eunice Kim!" I still remember the day your picture was in the paper, on the front page. My dad came to me with the paper folded in half, with your face big as that. And you had all these medals draped around your neck — I thought you were going to fall over. You were holding this trophy that looked to be about a foot taller than you. My dad goes, "Look at this!" And he rattles the paper in my face and says, "Eunice Kim's parents, very proud." Then he looked at me accusingly, narrowed his eyes and just said, "Electric guitar."
EUNICE. You play guitar?
PAUL. I tried. My parents hated it, they never even learned the terminology. My mom kept referring to my amp as "the loud thing" — she'd be like, "Turn off that loud thing!" And my dad, my dad usually referred to my guitar as "the devil's instrument." That gave me immense satisfaction.
EUNICE. I can't believe I don't remember you.
PAUL. About this high? Bowl haircut? It was not a good time in my life.
EUNICE. I guess I didn't know that many kids my age.
PAUL. Ah, you were busy practicing and winning. I mean, I guess that was the thing. I wanted to hate you, but I couldn't. I heard you play once.
EUNICE. You did?
PAUL. My younger sister, poor thing got drafted to play the viola. She started competing and of course the whole family got dragged out to support. I remember sitting there, just wanting to slit my wrists. I mean, the kids were good, but classical music makes me feel like I'm listening to one long Suzuki lesson on tape over and over again, you know?

And then you came out. I can't even remember what you were playing, but it was stunning. I felt like you were slowly hammering these little nails in my heart one by one. It was amazing.

EUNICE. Wait. You were Hannah's brother, weren't you?
PAUL. Yup. Still am.
EUNICE. She was good. Nice too, would say hi and smile.
PAUL. You don't play anymore, do you?
EUNICE. No.
PAUL. I always wondered what happened. Why'd you stop? Was it the pressure?
EUNICE. No, no one ever made me play. I wanted to. I loved it. *(An uncomfortable pause.)*
PAUL. I'm sorry, I really don't mean to pry. Man, if Emmy were here, she'd kill me. She always says I'm too nosy.
EUNICE. Who's Emmy?
PAUL. My fiancée.
EUNICE. You're engaged?
PAUL. Two months.
EUNICE. Wow.
PAUL. How 'bout you?
EUNICE. Oh, it was an immaculate conception. He's long gone.
PAUL. I'm sorry.
EUNICE. Yeah. Why do you think you got the dinner invite?
PAUL. Oh, man. No *wonder* you looked at me like you wanted to kill me.
EUNICE. Nothing personal —
PAUL. Are you kidding? I'm flattered that your mom thinks I'm good enough for you.
EUNICE. I think if you're Korean with a pulse you're good enough.
PAUL. No, your mom thinks the world of you.
EUNICE. She does?
PAUL. Yeah, she's always like, "Eunice is so bright, so smart, she could be anything if she just put her mind to it … "
EUNICE. That does sound like her. When did you know? I mean, how did you know she was the one?
PAUL. I don't know. I mean, I've been in love before where I'm just so excited whenever that person walks into a room that it's like they *are* the room. But with Emmy, it's kind of different. Calmer. Better. I mean, the way she explains it, you don't marry someone because you're in love. You marry someone because it's a good match, because you make a good team.
EUNICE. Sounds unromantic.
PAUL. What's romantic? Being swept off your feet and then having

it burn out in a year? Didn't your parents ever tell you about chung?
EUNICE. What?
PAUL. It's a form of love. But it's not like our idea of love. It's like care ... I don't know how to describe it. In fact, Emmy says I really don't understand what it is and that I can't because I'm not really Korean — you know, born there and everything.
EUNICE. You mean, you can't feel it if you're not?
PAUL. Well, if you don't have a word for something, then how can you? *(Pause.)* I have to admit, when your mom offered me dinner, I was hoping you'd be here. It's nice to finally meet you.
EUNICE. Disappointing, huh?
PAUL. Not at all. You know, after that competition where I saw you, I went home and dug up that newspaper. I put your face up on my wall.
EUNICE. You're kidding.
PAUL. I mean, it wasn't like a creepy stalker thing, I just liked it. Liked your smile. Because you know what? You had every right to smile and be proud of your medals and trophies. You were good, really good. I've never been half as good as that at anything.
EUNICE. I bet you're a good doctor.
PAUL. As a matter of fact, I am. *(A small and comfortable silence.)* Here. It's the last one. Eat. *(He takes his chopsticks and puts food on her plate. Paul disappears.)*
EUNICE. Also on the reading list: Tennessee Williams' *The Glass Menagerie*. Pay special attention to the Gentleman Caller: the long-awaited and hoped-for someone that is never quite what we expect, and is never something we can have. *(Sah-Jin is clearing the table angrily. Eunice helps her.)* It's not my fault.
SAH-JIN. You didn't even try. Don't you see? It could be the perfect solution to everything. He is what you need, someone steady and secure. And then you could keep the baby, Eunice. Just think —
EUNICE. Is that what this is about?
SAH-JIN. I just thought that maybe if you had a husband, then you could — You wouldn't have to hide anything, Eunice, and the baby wouldn't be ashamed —
EUNICE. You mean, *you* wouldn't be.
SAH-JIN. I only try to do what's best for you. What your father would want. My intentions, they are good.
EUNICE. I know. That's always been the problem.
SAH-JIN. I'm just saying, you could've been nicer.

EUNICE. Ma, he's engaged.
SAH-JIN. It's not serious.
EUNICE. He *loves* her, they've got chung, or whatever.
SAH-JIN. What?
EUNICE. Chung. Chung!
SAH-JIN. Oh, *chung*.
EUNICE. Yeah, that. So what is it?
SAH-JIN. It's impossible to explain. You wouldn't understand.
EUNICE. It's love, right?
SAH-JIN. Puh! What's love? Love is nothing.
EUNICE. Is it commitment? Devotion? Destiny?
SAH-JIN. Stop talking nonsense. You don't have to love someone to have chung with them. You don't even need to like them to have chung with them. Put it this way: you could have chung with someone you hate.
EUNICE. That doesn't make sense.
SAH-JIN. Think about it: you hate someone, he's like a shadow that falls across your life. Now take that person away. You feel this emptiness, this feeling that something in your life, something is missing. Where's your shadow? What's proving you are there? Something that helped make you who you are is gone. That's chung. It's love, but not quite love. Love, but more than love.
EUNICE. That's not chung, that's co-dependency.
SAH-JIN. No. Chung is when you give the other person whatever it is in your power to give them. Whatever they ask. Because you care for them so much.
EUNICE. Can you feel it for someone instantly? Like chung at first sight?
SAH-JIN. It's not passion. Chung takes time.
EUNICE. Have you ever loved anyone, the way I mean?
SAH-JIN. Like love you fall in? I don't think so.
EUNICE. Really? Never? Not even once?
SAH-JIN. So what. You have.
EUNICE. Yes.
SAH-JIN. And has it helped you? *(Eunice makes no attempt to answer.)* Love goes, passion goes. But chung stays.

Scene 4

Eunice writes the letter.

EUNICE. My parents were old when they met. Old for their day and time. He was thirty; she was twenty-nine. A year after they married, they came here with nothing and opened and closed every kind of business you can think of. Liquor store, drycleaning. And then they opened a convenience store, open from eight to eleven, six days a week. They worked together in that store for five years until the day my father was shot. My mother, to this day, has never talked about what happened. Even though she was the one who called the ambulance and sat with my father as he died. When I was in junior high, I saw that famous film of Kennedy's assassination in history class. And ever since then, in my head, when I think back on that day, I imagine my father is Kennedy and my mom is Jacqueline. *(As Eunice talks, dim lights come up on two vague figures dressed as Jacqueline and John F. Kennedy. They are sitting as if in a car. They reenact the shooting from the Zapruder film, soundlessly, over and over again. Underneath the following, the sound of whispering begins to rise but it is impossible to make out the words.)* When the bullet strikes him, he has no idea what has happened. He is more surprised than in pain. When he falls over on her, she screams over and over again. His blood stains her pink suit. His blood stains her hands. And she will never be clean again. *(Lights on the figures snap off as lights go up on the Girl. She holds her head in her hands and rocks. Her words are still whispered, but now are audible.)*
GIRL. Get up please please please just get up and say something please just get up and do something get up please please please just get up GET UP. *(Lights go out on the girl and simultaneously up on Sah-Jin, who is in bed.)*
SAH-JIN. Who's there? Eunice? *(Eunice stands at Sah-Jin's doorway, hesitating.)*
EUNICE. Can I sleep here?
SAH-JIN. What's wrong?
EUNICE. Bad dreams.

SAH-JIN. Come. *(Eunice dives into Sah-Jin's bed like a little girl.)* Bad dreams about?
EUNICE. I don't remember. Just bad. I don't want to stay in that room, Ma.
SAH-JIN. Don't be silly. Bad dreams can't hurt you. Here, scratch my back. *(She turns her back towards Eunice. Eunice begins scratching it.)*
EUNICE. Ma, why'd you come here? You and Dad?
SAH-JIN. What kind of stupid question is that? You wish you had growed up in Korea? You know over there, department stores, whole department stores, just fall down for no reason. And on the street, no one stops for red lights, it's true. If there's no one around, they just go right through. Is that the kind of country you want to grow up in?
EUNICE. That's not what I mean. I just wonder sometimes why you came here. I don't think Dad even liked it here. I remember how it felt after the store, after — *(Sah-Jin moves away from Eunice.)*
SAH-JIN. Why are you thinking of that?
EUNICE. I don't know, I —
SAH-JIN. Eunice, you weren't even there. You have no idea how terrible, if you did, you wouldn't be bringing it up.
EUNICE. But maybe if we talked about it, it wouldn't be so —
SAH-JIN. What good does talk do? Doesn't bring anyone back. Doesn't change anything. Why don't you go back to your room. I can't sleep with you in my bed. You kick me in your sleep. *(Sah-Jin gets up.)* Here. I'll make you some tea. You want some tea? *(Eunice notices something in the corner of the room.)*
EUNICE. What is that?
SAH-JIN. Oh, I took it out of your room. Before you came. *(Eunice gets up and looks at it. It's a cello case.)* What's wrong with you? It doesn't bite.
EUNICE. I thought you got rid of it.
SAH-JIN. I tried to. I couldn't.
EUNICE. I was talented, wasn't I?
SAH-JIN. You were the best.
EUNICE. Better than … better than …
SAH-JIN. Yes. You were. *(Sah-Jin leaves. Eunice goes to the cello case and looks at it for a moment. Then she picks it up and stuffs it into Sah-Jin's crowded closet. A box falls down and Eunice picks it up. It falls partly open. Sah-Jin enters. Eunice hides the box behind her back.)* Water will be done soon.
EUNICE. I don't want any. I'll be fine.

SAH-JIN. Where's the…?
EUNICE. I put it away. In there. *(She starts to leave.)* G'night.
SAH-JIN. Char-ja. Eunice? *(Eunice turns.)* Just go to bed. All this thinking … I tell you too much is no good.

Scene 5

Eunice's room. Eunice examines the box. It's made of a dark, glossy wood. There's an ornate latch that has grown dull with age. Eunice opens the box.

WOMAN. A photo of a young woman. *(The woman appears. Flash.)*
EUNICE. Oh my God. Ma.
WOMAN. One watch with a faded face and a gold band. Stopped at 11:22. *(She holds up a watch and then slips it on.)* One scarf, square, colorful. *(She holds up the scarf and ties it around her head.)*
DANIEL. A photo of a young man. *(Daniel appears. Flash.)* A book of postcards of California. Blank. Never sent. *(He holds up the book and lets it fall open. It's folded like an accordion.)*
WOMAN. And a book.
DANIEL. *Letters to a Young Poet* by Rainer Maria Rilke.
WOMAN. Signed —
DANIEL. Daniel.

Scene 6

Lights up on Sah-Jin, in the kitchen. She is peeling garlic in a bowl of water. Eunice has the box open in front of her.

EUNICE. I don't understand why you're getting so upset.
SAH-JIN. I am not upset.

EUNICE. You were so beautiful.
SAH-JIN. I was okay.
EUNICE. Look — who's that? The guy.
SAH-JIN. The name, I can't even remember.
EUNICE. Try Daniel.
SAH-JIN. What?
EUNICE. He signed this book — see?
SAH-JIN. Yes, Daniel. That was it.
EUNICE. He gave you a book and his photo and you don't remember?
SAH-JIN. It was a long time ago.
EUNICE. I know you don't have Alzheimer's, Ma, so stop acting like you do. *(She points to the photo.)* Look at him. Look at his face. I know you remember.
SAH-JIN. He was an American. I think. Come to our village.
EUNICE. Were you seeing him?
SAH-JIN. Don't disrespect your father.
EUNICE. I'm not. I'm just asking.
SAH-JIN. I hardly knew him.
EUNICE. But you were friends.
SAH-JIN. Everyone knew him, who he was. He was with the church. And he was the strangest-looking man we'd ever seen. So tall and all arms and legs and. He'd stop by every once in a while, that's all. Say hello.
EUNICE. So why keep the book?
SAH-JIN. You think I don't read or something?
EUNICE. Could you stop peeling garlic for just one second? You know they have whole jars of ready-peeled garlic at the supermarket.
SAH-JIN. You think that makes food taste good?
EUNICE. Look. *(She puts her hand on her mother's to make her stop.)* What does this say? *(She points to the title page of the book.)* The Korean.
SAH-JIN. It says "To Teacher," okay?
EUNICE. So was he one of your piano students, back in Korea?
SAH-JIN. Yes, that's how we knew each other. I taught him a little piano. He taught me a little English. Like a trade. That's why he gave me the book. He was only there for five or six months. Then he left, went back to the States.
EUNICE. How come you never mentioned him before?
SAH-JIN. What are you, some pot calling bigger pot black?

EUNICE. What?
SAH-JIN. You never mention who is the one — *(She nods meaningfully at Eunice's stomach.)*
EUNICE. That's different. I don't talk about it because it's not important.
SAH-JIN. Exactly. Same thing. What I don't say, I don't say because it is not important.

Scene 7

EUNICE. Rilke's *Letters to a Young Poet*. Written by the great German poet to a young man who is now forever known as "My Dear Mr. Kappus."

When she was young, my mother was the most beautiful woman our family had seen in generations. Her hair wasn't like mine; it wasn't a thin and mousy brownish, a black that hadn't quite made up its mind yet; her hair shone the deepest, quietest black imaginable. She used to wear it down all the time … when I was a child, she'd let me brush it and I can still feel it, how it slipped through my hands and crackled with static. *(Sah-Jin appears, partly in shadow, her back to the audience. Little by little she takes down her hair.)*

After my father died, my mother started wearing her hair pulled back and it was like she had grown old and ageless at the same time. To this day, she has almost no wrinkles. I'm convinced it is the sheer tension of that bun that gives her a permanent face-lift. I used to go into the bathroom in the evening, after she'd already gone to sleep and see a huge pile of black hairpins on the sink. It was like she was held together by them. All of her, held together by little pieces of twisted and bent steel. *(The woman has taken Sah-Jin's place. She turns and faces the audience. Eunice looks at the book carefully. She turns it in her hand and looks closer.)* And … margin notes?
EUNICE and WOMAN.

Say you hate me say
you do
stop here
and I lost my

WOMAN.

You must not understand me

(As the woman speaks, she slowly moves forward and the bedroom is transformed.)

Say you hate me
must not
must not
must not
must not
Do Say you do
Good day
A day
Goodness
Goodness
Memory
Memory
I will
So much

(The walls become white and opaque, illuminated by a soft glow, so that they look like rice paper walls. There is a small piano. There are flat, square pillows on the ground and a short dark red table. The woman keeps speaking the margin notes until the set is complete.)

EUNICE. Where are we?

WOMAN. Look around. Somewhere between the historical TV dramas you've seen and modern soaps set in Seoul, you have conjured up this place. Somewhere in the middle of five thousand years, there is this room.

EUNICE. Is this where you grew up?

WOMAN. Yes, but look outside.

EUNICE. It looks like … Southern California.

WOMAN. Where *you* grew up. What you imagine is always from what you know.

EUNICE. Aren't rice paper walls medieval?

WOMAN. Yes, but they look so nice and you can't help it: you like things zen. *(The woman sits at the piano and starts playing.)*

EUNICE. What is this?

WOMAN. This is the story of the what happened, or even better, of the what never happened — which, I might add, is far more interesting. *(Daniel appears outside the house. He hears the piano and stops and listens.)*

EUNICE. Who is that?
WOMAN. Daniel.
EUNICE. Who is *that*?
WOMAN. You'll see.
EUNICE. He's beautiful.
WOMAN. So am I. *(Daniel approaches the house as the woman plays. In the following scene, when Daniel speaks, he speaks hesitantly and awkwardly. The woman speaks perfectly. They are speaking in Korean.)*
DANIEL. Hello? Person home is? *(He stands at the doorway, listening. The song ends.)* Please. Don't stop. It is too pretty. *(The woman stands up, startled. She bows.)*
WOMAN. Is there something I may help Mr. Merritt with?
DANIEL. I come to learn. *(He gestures to the piano.)* You teach, yes?
WOMAN. Yes, but only to children.
DANIEL. Teach me.
WOMAN. I'm sorry, I can't. Now if Mr. Merritt will excuse me …
DANIEL. Please. I will pay.
WOMAN. I couldn't possibly —
DANIEL. Not with money. With English.
WOMAN. English?
DANIEL. Yes. I will teach you. For piano lessons, I am happy. Start now? *(A long pause.)*
WOMAN. What does Mr. Merritt know already? *(He smiles.)*
DANIEL. Not a thing. *(He sits at the piano.)*
WOMAN. All right then: this is middle C. Every key is a different note. C-D-E-F-G-A-B-C. Eight notes make a scale. And it repeats itself, all the way up the keys. *(She plays a C-major scale for Daniel, crossing over so that she goes across several octaves.)*
DANIEL. I see. Like English alphabet. *(The woman repeats just the eight-note scale, playing it up and then down.)*
WOMAN. C-major scale. *(She gestures for him to try it. Daniel slowly and awkwardly plays the scale.)*
DANIEL. Do you know writer, Virginia Woolf? She writes human mind is made like a thing, like one of these. Like a piano. Except it goes A to Z. How to say? You can go easy from A to R, maybe S, these notes our mind can reach. But more difficult with every next letter.
WOMAN. What do the notes represent?
DANIEL. Anything. If C-scale is A, then the song you play when I come in, maybe M or N. And someday I reach, can play that

song, but then there is still harder and harder songs. X is maybe Chopin or Rachmaninoff. See?

WOMAN. And there's always some point farther away. Like chasing the horizon.

DANIEL. Yes. Z, no one ever reach. Impossible to reach. *(He slowly plays the scale up and down, then chord progressions, arpeggios — all the standard piano lesson fare.)*

WOMAN. *(To Eunice.)* I'd never had a more diligent student. Or seen anyone with hair so light. In the sun, his arms were dusted with gold. It wasn't until much later that he told me that he never cared to learn the piano at all. He just wanted to be close to me because my hair was the most beautiful thing he had ever seen. *(She reaches over Daniel's shoulder to correct his hand position. He stops playing and turns toward her.)*

DANIEL. Why do you tie back? *(He loosens her hair and lets it fall forward. He takes it in his hands, slowly feeling its texture. He gathers some of it and shapes it into a brush, which he then runs along her arm.)*

WOMAN. Tickles.

DANIEL. Don't move. I painting your hand. And your arm. Your face. *(He runs the pointed tip of her hair lightly along her face. She closes her eyes.)*

WOMAN. Don't. Daniel. Don't. *(She opens her eyes.)*

DANIEL. You should wear down. Always. *(Daniel is still and the lights on him dim.)*

EUNICE. Were you in love with him?

WOMAN. That's not the right question.

EUNICE. What is the right question?

WOMAN. Some people, you meet them and they take your whole world and do this: *(She holds her hands out as if she's holding something and tilts it askew.)* He came, took my world, the world that had always felt wrong, and he did this: *(She rights her hands.)* That's the answer.

EUNICE. But what's the question for that? *(Daniel steals up behind the woman and puts his hands over her eyes.)*

WOMAN. Hello, Daniel.

DANIEL. How you know?

WOMAN. Because of how you smell.

DANIEL. I do? Bad?

WOMAN. Just different. Like *(Sniffs him.)* wood. Right ... *(Stops near his face.)* there.

DANIEL. Oh, aftershave.

WOMAN. After what?
DANIEL. Put it on after. *(Mimes shaving.)* Every day.
WOMAN. *(In wonder.)* Every day.
DANIEL. Look: *(He takes out the book of postcards from his bag and shows them to the woman.)* Hollywood. See? And Santa Monica Pier. That is big wheel. Person ride. You can see forever.
WOMAN. Say the names again.
DANIEL. Bel Air. Malibu. Santa Monica. Brentwood, Beverly Hills …
WOMAN. Beautiful. *(The woman looks at the postcards again.)* This is California?
DANIEL. Yes.
WOMAN. And is it really this beautiful?
DANIEL. *(Looking at her.)* Yes. I brought something else. For you. To thank. For lessons. *(He takes the book out and gives it to her.)*
WOMAN. *Letters to a Young Poet*?
DANIEL. From more old and more great poet. You will like.
WOMAN. Will you sign it for me?
DANIEL. Of course. *(He takes a pen out and signs the book.)* To Teacher. Daniel. *(He is gone. Eunice takes the scarf and puts it into her hair.)*
EUNICE. For everything there is a reason.
WOMAN. If you just go back far enough, you can find it.
EUNICE. He said —
WOMAN. Come with me.
EUNICE. I said, Yes.
WOMAN. Even though my mother says —
EUNICE. These Americans have big noses and they smell like milk. Even though everyone says —
WOMAN. This is infatuation. Your life with him will be built on air.
EUNICE. I don't listen. I don't care. The new world, bright like Sundays, vast as water. Oh, I can hardly wait!
WOMAN. He fills my emptinesses —
EUNICE. And I know we love each other.
WOMAN. So much.
EUNICE. And we have chung?
WOMAN. Maybe. Yes. We were
EUNICE. I was — in love. My whole life, I held myself apart. I thought I was not capable or worthy —
WOMAN. Or ready.

EUNICE. And then it came to me. *(The woman disappears into the dark. Joe emerges holding a long box, the kind that looks like it holds long-stemmed roses.)*
JOE. Open it.
EUNICE. Please tell me you didn't.
JOE. It's not a big deal. Just open it.
EUNICE. You can't keep giving me gifts like this. *(Eunice opens the box and gasps.)* Oh my God. *(She lifts out a drapery rod.)*
JOE. You've had that string with a blanket over it hanging in front of your window ever since I've known you. It's time you had a real window treatment.
EUNICE. I can't believe you even know the term "window treatment."
JOE. I'll help you put it up.
EUNICE. Where have you been all my life?
JOE. In Vermont, mainly.
EUNICE. I'll cherish it forever, or at least until my next apartment.
JOE. Actually, I wanted to talk to you about that. My lease is up in a few months; I just know they're going to crank up the rent.
EUNICE. I hate that.
JOE. Yeah, but I was thinking that maybe I'd try to find another place. I feel like I've kinda outgrown that little studio anyway.
EUNICE. But there's no way you can afford a one-bedroom.
JOE. I could if I split it with someone. *(Pause.)*
EUNICE. You want to move in together?
JOE. You know, when I rehearsed this scene beforehand, I imagined those words coming out of your mouth with a much more upbeat tone.
EUNICE. I just. Didn't see it coming. Moving in. I never had anyone before, or even came close to — Wow.
JOE. So does that mean … yes?
EUNICE. Joe, how well do you think you know me?
JOE. I know it's you on the phone in half a word. I know you hate shellfish. I know you keloid. What else is there?
EUNICE. I don't want to move in with you.
JOE. That's okay. You don't have to. It was just a thought. But. Do you mean now or ever?
EUNICE. Why would you want to move in with someone like me?
JOE. Someone like what?
EUNICE. Someone who, someone who doesn't know how.

JOE. What are you talking about?
EUNICE. It's like … I want to, and it's there, but I can't, I can't —
JOE. Can't what? Do you love me?
EUNICE. You know I do —
JOE. No. You always say, "I love being with you." Or, "You make me so happy." But you never just say it. Can't you just say it? *(Silence.)*
EUNICE. Joe. It's not that I don't want to settle down, it's just that I can't picture myself — I mean, I don't think I'm built for that.
JOE. Well. I am. *(Joe is gone. Eunice slips the scarf out of her hair. She is alone. No more imaginary Korea.)*

Scene 8

EUNICE. Another item for the reading list, D. H. Lawrence's story "The Rocking-Horse Winner." A little boy lives in a house that whispers, *Money, there must be more money*. In order to stop the whispering, he takes to riding his rocking horse endlessly, hours and hours each day. Well, I'm going to tell you a story about a girl. Her house had whisperings of its own, and her rocking horse was her cello. She was six when she touched it for the first time and as soon as she touched it, she was good. And then with time, she became great. The life she had before she began playing is silent, unremarkable. But when she played … *(The girl appears. She begins playing.)* When she played, she was extraordinary. Nothing was beyond her reach. She wasn't afraid of anything. Ten years old and she didn't even know what fear was. After her father died, she started playing the cello as she had never played before. By the age of fifteen, she was a champion. *(The music stops. The girl stops, frozen, completely lost in her own thoughts.)* And then. Everything. Changed. *(Sah-Jin appears. The girl doesn't even look at her.)*
SAH-JIN. Eunice. Eunice, it's me.
GIRL. I know who you are.
SAH-JIN. I brought you food.
EUNICE. I don't want it.
SAH-JIN. You're hungry, I know you are. Why won't you eat?
GIRL. Might be poisoned.
SAH-JIN. How can you even think that?

GIRL. I'm just being careful. After all, how do I know you aren't working for them? They didn't shoot *you*, did they? *(Sah-Jin slaps the girl.)*

They said you'd do that.

SAH-JIN. "They" don't exist! If you say the word "they" one more time, I'm going to scream.

GIRL. Then scream.

SAH-JIN. I brought you your medicine, if you just take the pills, you'll see — *(The girl bats the pills out of Sah-Jin's hand. Sah-Jin scrambles to collect them.)*

GIRL. Those pills make me stupid! So that I won't suspect, won't be on to them.

SAH-JIN. On to what? None of this is real. You are just imagining.

GIRL. Oh, Ma. Reality is like an onion. There are so many layers. You have no idea. *(Lights shift. Sah-Jin is gone. The girl turns towards Eunice.)* And then — you remember this part, don't you? And then what happened?

EUNICE. I don't know, it was a long time ago —

GIRL. *(Mimicking Eunice.)* I know you don't have Alzheimer's, so stop acting like you do. C'mon.

EUNICE. He spoke to her, to me. I thought God, or something, was speaking to me.

GIRL. You found God, or He found you. And He said that they were after you. The men who killed your father.

EUNICE. They were going to kill me.

GIRL. And you believed Him. So for six months you lived out there in the wilds of L.A. County suburbia. Hiding behind the Alpha Beta. Roaming the La Puente Hills Mall. Like a latter-day John the Baptist. L.A.'s a good place to be a runaway. No fear of freezing to death that's for sure. But you never strayed very far from home. Why is that?

EUNICE. Because He told me not to.

GIRL. And what else? What else did he tell you to do?

EUNICE. I don't remember.

GIRL. Yes, you do.

EUNICE. He said —

GIRL. Go to the house. Go when it's quiet.

EUNICE. Why should I go back there?

GIRL. So that I can take the pain from you. That's what you want, isn't it?

EUNICE. I don't know.
GIRL. All you have to do is go back there and finish what has already begun.
EUNICE. You want me to — ?
GIRL. Think about it. She's miserable and unhappy anyway. Hasn't she been through enough pain? Really, you'd be doing her a favor. Heaven is paradise, Eunice. Don't you want your mom to be with your father in paradise? *(The scratchy sound of a recorded cello rises. Lights go up on Sah-Jin. She is sitting, listening to the music.)*
EUNICE. I go to the house.
GIRL. That's right. Go on.
EUNICE. I go from window to window and no one seems to be home. And then I find her in the living room. Listening to some old Casals record. She looks old and tired and oh my God she is beautiful in that room. I see a hand on the windowsill. It moves the curtain. And then I realize, it's my hand. *(The girl enters the room.)*
SAH-JIN. Eunice! *(Sah-Jin goes to the girl and embraces her. Eunice remains in the dark, absolutely still.)* You scare me to death. What's wrong with you, you're not dressed for the cold at all! Don't listen to me, I don't care, I'm just glad you're home. *(The girl disentangles herself from her mother's arms.)*
GIRL. I'm not home to stay. I just needed something.
SAH-JIN. Temperature's getting lower. You should just stay here. At least for the night.
GIRL. You're not listening to me. I'm not staying.
SAH-JIN. Then what? Are you hungry? Do you need money? *(The girl is clearly distracted, but she struggles to act as if everything's normal.)*
GIRL. *(Low.)* Sshhh!
SAH-JIN. What?
GIRL. No, not money. What are you listening to?
SAH-JIN. Oh, this … it's silly, I know. But it helps me not to miss you so much. *(Sah-Jin lifts the needle off the record and the cello music stops.)* House gets so quiet. You can't imagine. Without you playing. It's been so long. I keep the cello right where you left it, but now, it just collects dust. *(The cello is propped up in the corner of the room. The girl walks over to the cello. She slowly sits and begins playing, uncertainly at first, and then with more speed and fluidity. She plays the prelude to Bach's First Cello Suite in G. The girl suddenly stops. She looks at her hands. Eunice looks at her hands.)* What is it?
GIRL. *(Touching her fingertips.)* Hurts.

SAH-JIN. Keep playing. It will go away.
GIRL. I sound awful.
SAH-JIN. You sound beautiful.
GIRL. Bach would turn over in his grave.
SAH-JIN. Someday you will be better than Bach.
GIRL. Don't be ridiculous.
SAH-JIN. Better than Casals. Better than Yo-Yo Ma.
GIRL. Maybe.
SAH-JIN. You can be anything you want. If you don't get what you want …
SAH-JIN and GIRL. … it just means you didn't want it bad enough.
SAH-JIN. Then again. *(The girl continues playing. She starts to near the end of the prelude and the music begins to crescendo. The notes climb higher and higher. But this time she struggles. One wrong note shrieks out and then another.)* Eunice? *(The music gets more and more jarring, more and more violent. Eunice and the girl both clasp their hands over their ears.)*
GIRL. NO. Shut up!
SAH-JIN. What, what is it?
GIRL. Stop it. LEAVE ME ALONE.
SAH-JIN. I don't see anything, I'm — I don't understand. Who's there — who are you talking to? *(The girl stands, knocking the cello to the ground. It falls with a terrible clatter.)*
GIRL. Can't you hear them, Um-mah? Make them stop!
SAH-JIN. Just tell me who, who's hurting you? *(The girl seems to be struggling with herself.)*
EUNICE. No I won't No I won't No I won't No I won't *(Eunice continues speaking under the girl, getting louder and louder.)*
GIRL. No I WON'T
SAH-JIN. Eunice, what's happening? WHO'S HURTING YOU? *(The girl lifts her bow with one hand high over her head, her fist tightly encircling it. Her other hand she lays flat on the ground. She drives the end of the bow down into her hand and cries out.)* EUNICE. *(Blackout except for one faint light on Eunice. She is still crouched over. Beat. She slowly uncurls and sits up. She raises her hand and looks at it.)*

End of Act One

ACT TWO

Scene 1

An office. Paul is examining Eunice's arm.

EUNICE. Thanks for squeezing me in like this.
PAUL. No problem — today's not so busy. This looks fine. If it gets fuzzy around the edges, then let me know. You've probably had this mole for years. What made you want to get it checked out now?
EUNICE. Oh, I don't know.
PAUL. Because as long as you don't notice any — *(He looks at her face.)* This isn't why you're here, is it?
EUNICE. Well, it's not the *only* reason why I'm here —
PAUL. You know, normal people just call and say, "Hey, want to have coffee?"
EUNICE. I know.
PAUL. Is everything okay?
EUNICE. Yeah. It's just that I don't have my check-up until next week and there were just some questions I had now. And I thought maybe you could. Illuminate them.
PAUL. All right. Shoot.
EUNICE. Are there any diseases that are, you know, hereditary?
PAUL. Well, sure. Lots of them. I mean it ranges from semi-hereditary, like psoriasis or something, to —
EUNICE. But is there any way to know what the probabilities are? Exactly? Like say I had a history of diabetes in my family. Could I calculate the chances of my baby having diabetes?
PAUL. But there's no sure thing. I mean, some of it is genetics, yes. But a lot of it is environment. It's not smoking, it's exercising, it's the choices you make.
EUNICE. Right.
PAUL. You're just getting nervous, it's natural. It's going to be fine. Your baby's going to be fine.
EUNICE. It's just there're so many factors …

PAUL. Listen to the worrier. Sound just like your mom.
EUNICE. Bite your tongue.
PAUL. Just enjoy it, will you? Go buy stuff. I don't know. Baby stuff, walkie-talkies, teething toys, whatever.
EUNICE. Oh, I'm not. I'm not keeping it.
PAUL. What?
EUNICE. I'm putting it up for adoption. That's why I came home.
PAUL. But your mom —
EUNICE. My mom what? Did she tell you I was keeping it?
PAUL. No, she didn't say anything. She just seemed so. Happy.
EUNICE. She did?
PAUL. Well. Yeah. Anyway. It's funny.
EUNICE. What?
PAUL. That you — I mean, Emmy and I, we can't have kids. And we want them. And here's you … Anyway.
EUNICE. You can't?
PAUL. Well, she can't … no.
EUNICE. I'm sorry. *(Paul shrugs.)*
PAUL. What're ya gonna do? You love who you love, right? So. Gotta get back to the suffering masses. Take two pills and call me in the morning.
EUNICE. Thank you.
PAUL. For what? Tell your mom I said hi, okay?
EUNICE. Hey, Paul?
PAUL. Yeah?
EUNICE. Just out of curiosity, what could leave a scar, like a star-shaped one? Here? *(She touches her throat.)*
PAUL. Sounds like a trache.
EUNICE. A what?
PAUL. A tracheotomy. Your airway gets blocked so they have to put a hole in you.
EUNICE. What?
PAUL. Don't look so horrified. You talking about your mom's scar? That's ancient.
EUNICE. What do you mean?
PAUL. Probably a childhood bout with pneumonia or something. I wouldn't worry about it. Remember: normal people: phone, coffee. Much easier.

Scene 2

Sah-Jin is sitting with a tape player on her lap. Her eyes are closed and she's listening to a piece of cello music. Eunice enters.

EUNICE. Ma? What're you doing?
SAH-JIN. Nothing. How was the mall? Find anything good?
EUNICE. No.
SAH-JIN. Are you sleeping okay? I can you hear you at night. Tossing, turning.
EUNICE. If you can hear me, then it means you're not sleeping well either. *(She stops the tape.)* Ma. Can I ask you something? How'd you get the scar? The one on your throat?
SAH-JIN. Why're you asking about that?
EUNICE. Just curious.
SAH-JIN. I told you.
EUNICE. No, you didn't.
SAH-JIN. I got sick, they put a hole in so I could breathe.
EUNICE. How old were you?
SAH-JIN. I don't remember.
EUNICE. Someone puts a hole in your throat and you don't remember?
SAH-JIN. Maybe eight. Maybe nine. *(Pause.)*
EUNICE. It's not you, is it?
SAH-JIN. What?
EUNICE. In that photo. She doesn't have your scar. You just said that you were —
SAH-JIN. Oh, Eunice, I'm too tired for this.
EUNICE. Why did you tell me that woman was you?
SAH-JIN. I didn't tell you, you *wanted* to think it, so I let you.
EUNICE. What?
SAH-JIN. You get to be my age and it doesn't matter so much anymore. Who said what, who did what, who is who …
EUNICE. That's bull. Facts are facts. This woman, is she a relative?
SAH-JIN. No, just a friend of the family.
EUNICE. But she looks like you. Like us.

SAH-JIN. We all look alike a little.
EUNICE. I'm serious. Who is she?
SAH-JIN. No one.
EUNICE. She is NOT no one. That's a horrible thing to say.
SAH-JIN. Why are you get so excited? It seem to make you upset and I told you, that's no good for the baby.
EUNICE. *Stop saying that.* I don't care what's good for the fucking baby!
SAH-JIN. What is wrong with you? Calm down.
EUNICE. I'm not a child.
SAH-JIN. Then stop acting like one! Look at you: so irritated, moody. Like you used to be —
EUNICE. I am NOT like that anymore.
SAH-JIN. I just meant you shouldn't think so much. This woman, she was a friend of the family. A good friend. She looked after me when I was young. That's all. Her family move away and then we lose touch. But I keep the photo because it reminds me of her. And I keep it in the book because it's around that same time that I know her and I know Daniel. That's all it is. Sometimes the answer is that easy. Things don't have to be mystery. You look for things that aren't there.
EUNICE. Really?
SAH-JIN. Really. *(Pause.)*
EUNICE. You're lying.
SAH-JIN. I do not lie, I NEVER lie —
EUNICE. ALL YOU DO IS LIE. *(Eunice grabs the tape player and takes out the tape.)* You want the tape? Huh? Then tell me what this is all about.
SAH-JIN. EUNICE.
EUNICE. I'll rip it out, so help me God. *(Sah-Jin hesitates and Eunice quickly pulls out some of the tape.)*
SAH-JIN. DON'T! *(Eunice throws the tape down. Sah-Jin retrieves it.)* This is the only tape I have, the only one. Why are you like this?
EUNICE. Bitter?
SAH-JIN. Cruel. You don't tell me everything. I don't expect you to. You need somewhere to stay, you come home. You need food, I feed you. You are pregnant, I don't ask questions. I let you be a stranger to me because I know that's what you need.
EUNICE. You have no idea what I need!
SAH-JIN. What about me? Since the moment you walked into

this house all you care about is how bad *your* life is, how much *you've* suffered. And you come here and expect me to give you everything, as usual, no matter what it costs me.
EUNICE. I LOST EVERYTHING.
SAH-JIN. And what do you think I have? I lost more. I lost MORE. Because at least you have yourself. I never had myself. I just had you.
EUNICE. That's not my fault, you can't blame me for that.
SAH-JIN. And here you are, digging into my life, not caring what it means to me, at the same time, you conveniently forget everything that happened to you in this house, pretending like it happened to someone else, in another life, not brave enough to look at it for what it is, to look at yourself for what it is.
EUNICE. And what is that, Ma, what am I?
SAH-JIN. I don't know. Not anymore. I don't know where you've gone. *(She looks at the tape in her hands.)* I miss what you were so much, you don't know how much I miss it. When you played it was like something inside me — the wrong things breaking apart and coming together right. I see that in you, that girl inside you and you never let her out.
EUNICE. I can't. Don't you understand?
SAH-JIN. I only ever want to make you happy. But sometimes, I think that you don't know how to be happy. That you never choose it. It's right there, but you don't choose it. Instead, you choose the difficult thing, the hard thing. Like the past. The past is a hard thing.
EUNICE. Then let *me* choose. Don't decide for me. *(Pause.)*
SAH-JIN. That woman is my sister.
EUNICE. You told me she died when she was a child.
SAH-JIN. She got sick. It was not like here. No good hospitals, no good medicine, no good anything. The war left nothing. What they could not heal, they took away.
EUNICE. Where?
SAH-JIN. To a home. And then no one ever spoke of her again. When I think of her, I think of fruit. One, a pale yellow fruit with ridges the length of your hand. She would peel it so quickly, long, see-through strands of skin. She would slice it into long thin canoes for me because she knew I liked it. Fruit never tasted as good as when it came from her hand. And the last time I saw her, she gave me a red, orange fruit, that had leaves on it like a little hat. Something like a tomato. Not much juice, a hard sweetness. After eating it, my fingers were coated with a powder that had tiny edges. Like sand.

Like glass. I waved goodbye to her with glass on my hands. Not everyone's like you, Eunice. Not everyone gets better.
EUNICE. What are you saying, that she was — ? Was she. Was she like me?
SAH-JIN. Yes. No. You're different.
EUNICE. Ma, all this time, why didn't you ever say anything?
SAH-JIN. Why? What good does it do?
EUNICE. Ma. Were there others? Before her? Before me?
SAH-JIN. I don't know.
EUNICE. Yes, you do —
SAH-JIN. I'm not lying, honestly I do not know. We didn't talk about it like that. My mother, she died when I was young and I never knew *how* she died. Do you understand? No one would ever tell me. They just never said.
EUNICE. But it's possible that there were others. We don't know for sure, but there could have been —
SAH-JIN. Oh, Eunice, say it like that, *anything* is possible —
EUNICE. So even if Dad hadn't died, even if everything had been different, I would've still — ? *(Eunice starts laughing.)*
SAH-JIN. Stop.
EUNICE. Oh, come on, this is irony at its richest! Two parents who sacrifice everything for their child, who strive to give her only the best ... And I don't inherit language or culture, hell, I don't even inherit your *hair* or your looks. I inherit a *disease. (Eunice swallows her bitter laughter.)* That's my heirloom.
SAH-JIN. Do you think that's all we gave you?
EUNICE. What does the rest matter?
SAH-JIN. One time, when you were still just a very little girl, I got up late in the middle of the night and found you in the living room. I tried to be angry, but you look so small, sitting in the glow of the TV, your nightgown all blue. Like the little girl in that bad movie you made me watch.
EUNICE. *Poltergeist.*
SAH-JIN. Except no ghost, just a little Japanese girl playing the violin. She's not much older than you. She finishes and there's so much applause. And you turn and say to me, I'm going to be better than that. I'm going to be better than anyone. And for a while, you were. That is part of you. *(Eunice holds up her hand and flexes it stiffly. She shows Sah-Jin the scar.)*
EUNICE. So is this.

Scene 3

Sah-Jin is at the locked door of Eunice's room.

SAH-JIN. Are you hungry? I made food. Not bought. Your favorites. Eunice? What's wrong with you? Open the door. You have to eat. You don't have to talk, but you have to eat. It's been three days and you haven't eaten a thing. Eunice. Eunice? *(Softly.)* You're scaring me.

Scene 4

EUNICE. When week two hit with no period in sight, I bought eight tests from the Duane Reade. I drank a pot of coffee and did them all in a row. Ate up an entire Sunday. And still I couldn't believe it. So I went to the clinic so I could be positive and as it turned out … I was. The nurse asked if I'd need a counselor. She didn't find it funny when I said, "Fuck the counselor — I need a drink!" For two days, I felt … I was terrified, but there was this kind of amazement. I had felt so empty for so long and suddenly … I was a vessel. And I knew what it must have been like to be — not Columbus — but one of his ships, carrying all that hope, carrying all that expectation to the New World. But there is no New World. And I'm no Columbus. I want you to know, it's not that I didn't want you. But long after you leave my arms, everything in you will bear you back towards me. My dust on your heels, my … in you, rotting you from the inside out … And I won't. I won't do that to you. Because I did. I do. Love you, I mean. In my own way, I do. It's just that there is no one in my heart. Not even me.

Scene 5

Eunice is in the kitchen, standing before a pile of lemons on the table. Sah-Jin walks into the kitchen, sees Eunice and freezes.

SAH-JIN. There you are. I was looking for you.
EUNICE. So you found me.
SAH-JIN. What's all this?
EUNICE. The tree out back is bursting with them. They're dropping on the ground and rotting.
SAH-JIN. But what are you going to do with all of them?
EUNICE. I don't know. Make lemonade, I guess. *(Eunice starts cutting the lemons in half and squeezing them into a glass.)*
SAH-JIN. Your father planted that tree.
EUNICE. Don't know why. He didn't even like lemons.
SAH-JIN. He meant to plant something else, a different fruit. But they sold him the wrong tree and he didn't know it until the fruit came out.
EUNICE. Poor Dad. Always getting shafted by life.
SAH-JIN. Don't say that.
EUNICE. Why not? It's true. I guess you never know what you've planted until it comes up. *(She pounds the glass of juice back and sucks her breath in loudly through her teeth. Exhaling:)* Sheee-uh!
SAH-JIN. *(Overlapping.)* Eunice!
EUNICE. Goddamn, Ma, that's some bitter fruit!
SAH-JIN. Drink some water. *(She gets Eunice a cup.)* Crazy girl.
EUNICE. Don't call me that. *(Pause.)*
SAH-JIN. After I saw your door open, I start to look for you everywhere. Then I look for you in the garage. The car was warm. Did you go somewhere?
EUNICE. Uh-huh.
SAH-JIN. Where?
EUNICE. To the doctor's. Had my check-up.
SAH-JIN. Why didn't you say so? I could've driven you. What did they say? Baby healthy?
EUNICE. Yeah.

SAH-JIN. Then why do you look like that?
EUNICE. Well. I don't have AIDS.
SAH-JIN. Eunice, what is it?
EUNICE. I changed my mind. I'm not doing adoption.
SAH-JIN. What?
EUNICE. I checked and I'm still within the safe time.
SAH-JIN. What do you mean?
EUNICE. Well, after the first trimester, the procedure isn't as —
SAH-JIN. *Procedure?*
EUNICE. It's really for the best, when you think about it, given the chances of —
SAH-JIN. No, you CAN'T. I won't let you. Adoption is one thing, but this —
EUNICE. Ma, do you know the statistics? Do you have any idea?
SAH-JIN. I knew and I still wanted you.
EUNICE. Who's going to want a baby like this?
SAH-JIN. Then keep the child! Keep it like I kept you.
EUNICE. Why couldn't you have been brave and just gotten rid of me?
SAH-JIN. There was always a chance you wouldn't have it, just like I didn't.
EUNICE. *(Overlapping.)* But I did.
SAH-JIN. *(Overlapping.)* I was not afraid. Not of having you. Not of raising you.
EUNICE. I was sick. I could've hurt you. Don't you understand?
SAH-JIN. But you got help —
EUNICE. If that's what you want to call it. They carted me away and pumped me full of drugs and this stupid body of mine just kept going —
SAH-JIN. And you got better. And now you're fine —
EUNICE. Look at me, Mother. Look at my "*fine.*"
SAH-JIN. But it's in you, it's all in you —
EUNICE. No. That girl's gone. Do you know why she was so good?
SAH-JIN. What do you mean?
EUNICE. Do you remember when I started becoming a champion?
SAH-JIN. You were twelve.
EUNICE. It was the year after Dad died.
SAH-JIN. That year, you won every contest you entered. Every tournament. Every competition.
EUNICE. I did nothing but play. Eight hours a day.

SAH-JIN. You went from being a good player to being a great one. Juilliard wanted you. Everyone wanted you.
EUNICE. When I played, I thought of nothing. Cared about nothing. Saw nothing. Heard nothing. I was going to make his sacrifice worth it.
SAH-JIN. He didn't die for you.
EUNICE. No, it was worse. He *lived* for me and only me. You know when I played, it was the only time we ever talked. There are so many different kinds of languages that exist between a father and daughter. And we didn't know any of them. I used to watch him in the evenings, writing out the checks for my lessons, my bows, my music. I was horrified by the large amounts. Those dollars represented his minutes, hours … his whole life trickling down into units of cash that brought me teachers, instruments, accessories. It felt like blood money. What kind of world, Ma?
SAH-JIN. What do you mean?
EUNICE. I was there. At the store.
SAH-JIN. What are you talking about? *(Pause.)* You were at school.
EUNICE. No, I was there.
SAH-JIN. Eunice.
EUNICE. I remember: It's a half-day, a sunny half-day and I'm flying home so fast I don't even stop at the ice cream truck.
SAH-JIN. I was in the back … I didn't even hear you come in.
EUNICE. I'm going to spring out and surprise Dad because I've made it to state. The highest honor for someone in my age bracket and I know he'll be happy. He'll smile, he hasn't smiled in so long.
SAH-JIN. No.
EUNICE. He's helping a customer. Two men — no, they seem young, bodies like boys. They bark, they splinter, they break, and my father he is — and I don't make a sound — and my father he is — nothing has sound — The men run out and — My mother —
SAH-JIN. I heard, I saw, I saw him fall —
EUNICE. Nothing has sound — You claw by the counters towards him and — Hold his head, hold his head —
SAH-JIN. Just hold his head — I hear someone wailing — And it's me —
EUNICE. *(Fast and whispered.)* Get up please please please just get up and say something please just get up and do something get up please please please —
SAH-JIN. But he doesn't —

EUNICE. And I run, as hard and fast as I can still no sound everything quiet — I run away and I don't look back. *(Pause.)* And that quiet … I tried to fill it with music. I thought I could push out all the sadness like it was so much dusty air. If I could just play beautifully enough … I came so close, Ma.
SAH-JIN. To what?
EUNICE. To being someone. Who mattered.
SAH-JIN. You think the cello was what made you matter?
EUNICE. What else was there?
SAH-JIN. Eunice-ya. Listen. I told you I was never in love, not like you mean. And it's true. I know for sure that I never been falling in love with anyone. Not your father even. I loved him, but a different way. Not like how it is on TV where you have a deep love for someone and they are like your best friend, they go with you like a companion through your whole life. Kind of depressed me, you know? I thought, I will never know a great love. How sad, to go through your whole life and never experience a great love. But then I realize *you* are my great love. Because you are me, you are in me. And everywhere you go, it's like I'm there too. And my love for you is so big, sometimes I don't even know what to do with it. It's like my heart is beating outside my body and it's terrible not knowing how to keep it safe. That's what the ribcage is for, but what to do when your heart is walking all over the world without you? And I love you like this, not because of anything you did. Not because you were talented or good at something. I loved you like this as soon as you were born. I loved you like this *before* you were born. I loved you like this before I even knew what you were. You didn't have to earn it. Or repay it. It was always already there. You just had to see it. *(A moment.)* Seems funny to think now … Did I ever tell you? Tell you why I wanted you to play the cello?
EUNICE. What?
SAH-JIN. I chose it for you.
EUNICE. No, I chose it. I remember the room you took me to. How there were all of those instruments and you let me go one by one and choose the one I wanted. And it felt right, that's why I chose it.
SAH-JIN. It was just a kind of whim. I heard it for the first time when I was just a child. I'd never seen or heard anything like it before. It was from another world, a better one, the one, more than anything, that I wanted to see. And I did. For better or worse, I did.

Scene 6

Korea. Daniel sits playing the cello. He is smoking while he plays. The smoke curls up in opaque tendrils around him. A girl opens the door of the house and listens until he finishes. She is twelve. Daniel stops and takes a drag of his cigarette. He puts it out.

DANIEL. Hey. Come here. *(She hangs back. Daniel fishes out a pack of gum from his pocket.)* You like gum, don't you? *(She quickly moves forward and snatches the gum from his hand. She chews a stick greedily.)* Hey, hold on, you got to take the wrapper off first. I've seen you before, hanging around. Sah-Jin, right? *(The Young Sah-Jin nods.)* Boy, you sure look like her. Know who I am?
YOUNG SAH-JIN. *(With a strong accent.)* Daniel.
DANIEL. That's right. And I'm your sister's friend. *(Hopefully.)* Do you know where they've taken her? *(Pause.)* Didn't think so. *(She quietly approaches the cello.)* Go on, you can touch it. It doesn't bite. This is the bow. Hold it like this. No straight, the bow has to be flat on the string. And then you draw it across. *(He puts his hand on hers and guides the bow over the strings. A rich note pours out and she smiles for the first time.)* There. See? Not so hard. *(She draws the bow and a note squawks out.)* Okay, a little hard. I used to play for your sister all the time. Talk about music appreciation. I'd sit out here and play to her window — God, your parents hated me for that. *(He hands her the whole pack of gum.)* Here, have it all. I don't need it. I'm leaving tomorrow to go back to the land of gum. But will you do something for me? Stand in her room and let me play to you. It'll be like it used to be, like I'm playing for her. Will you let me do that? *(She nods. She goes inside, and sits down. Outside Daniel plays.)*

Scene 7

EUNICE. We took pictures of the wrong things, and we recorded the wrong events. We told the wrong stories, and we remembered the wrong memories. What has lasted is sadness; it will outlast flesh. What has lasted is forgetfulness; it wins over memory every time. But sometimes, in the blue hour, between midnight and dawn, I'll wake up and my hands will be alive, moving over an imaginary cello all by themselves. That's how strong the muscle memory is. And then I feel such loss … but as Rilke would say, "[Y]ou must not be frightened, dear Mr. Kappus, if a sadness rises up before you larger than any you have ever seen; if a restiveness, like light and cloud-shadows, passes over your hands and over all you do. You must think that something is happening with you, that life has not forgotten you, that it holds you in its hand; it will not let you fall." *(Eunice sits with the cello, holding it like it's an old, fragile friend. She holds the bow and draws it over the string. At first it squawks and then a pure, rich note rings out. She starts playing a simple melody, like someone rusty and out of practice. But the song still holds together, revealing something of the player she once was. Sah-Jin comes to the door and listens. She holds a photo. Eunice stops playing but doesn't look up.)* I can't remember the rest. My hands … they shake.
SAH-JIN. Still sounds beautiful to me. *(She holds up the photo.)* Look. I found. This is you.
EUNICE. I'm not even in it. It's just you and Dad.
SAH-JIN. Look harder. You were inside me then. In this *(She makes a motion back and forth between herself and Eunice.)* there was you. *(Sah-Jin kneels in front of Eunice and puts her ear to her stomach. She listens closely.)* It's a girl.
EUNICE. How can you tell?
SAH-JIN. I can hear her singing.
EUNICE. A girl. What's she singing?
SAH-JIN. Very old song. About mountains and rain.
EUNICE. Yeah, right. *(Sah-Jin begins to hum a melody. Eunice begins to hum it with her.)* I didn't even know … that I knew that.
SAH-JIN. Exactly.
EUNICE. Is mother's love a kind of chung?

SAH-JIN. Yes, a kind. Maybe the strongest kind. When you are with someone, first there is love. And time passes and then there can be hate. But after that, what is left is chung. You can't have chung with someone you've just met. There is memory in chung. There is time.
EUNICE. Is there history?
SAH-JIN. Mmhmm. Memory plus time. *(Sah-Jin sees the box on Eunice's desk. She looks in it and takes out the watch. She holds it carefully. Eunice watches her. Sah-Jin winds it up and puts her ear to it.)* Hunh. Still works.
EUNICE. What's this thing in your hair? Is that a…?
SAH-JIN. They call it a HairDini. I order off TV.
EUNICE. You're kidding.
SAH-JIN. Just twist it and you have a bun. No more hairpins. Saves a lot of time.
EUNICE. Oh, Ma. *(Sah-Jin goes to the mirror.)*
SAH-JIN. Feh. I've gotten so old.
EUNICE. I think you're beautiful. After all, aren't all the women in our family beautiful? *(Lights dim. Sah-Jin disappears. We hear the Bach prelude. Eunice gathers together her letters. She puts them into the box.)* One hope chest. *(The woman and girl appear. The music continues. It reaches the point where the music crescendos, but this time, instead of falling apart, the music effortlessly climbs and climbs. The woman begins speaking and then gradually the girl and Eunice join in.)*

WOMAN.		
Good day		
A day	GIRL.	
Goodness	Good day	EUNICE.
Goodness	A day	Good day
Memory	Goodness	A day
Memory	Goodness	Goodness
Memory	Memory	Goodness
Memory	Memory	Memory
Memory	Memory	Memory

(End to the prelude of Bach's First Cello Suite in G.)

End of Play

PROPERTY LIST

Cello (GIRL, DANIEL, EUNICE)
Pillow, shoebox with fancy, black high-heeled shoes (SAH-JIN)
Iron, ironing board, shirt (JOE)
Two ties (JOE)
Keys (EUNICE)
Paper, pen (EUNICE)
Chopsticks, food (PAUL and EUNICE)
Cello case (SAH-JIN)
Box with photo, watch, scarf, postcards, book (EUNICE)
Garlic, bowl of water, knife (SAH-JIN)
Piano (WOMAN)
Bag with postcards, book and pen (DANIEL)
Scarf (EUNICE)
Long box with curtain rod (JOE)
Food, pills (SAH-JIN)
Record player (SAH-JIN)
Tape player with cassette (SAH-HIN)
Lemons, knife, glass (EUNICE)
Cup of water (SAH-JIN)
Cigarette, gum (DANIEL)
Photo (SAH-JIN)
Box with watch (SAH-JIN)

SOUND EFFECTS

Cello music
Piano music